Lost Underground Stations

JOHN GLOVER

NOSTALGIA RAIL

First published by
Crécy Publishing Limited 2014

© Text: John Glover 2013
© Photographs: As credited;
tickets from the Peter Waller collection

A CIP record for this book is available from the British Library

ISBN 9781908 347176

Printed in Malta by Melita Press

Nostalgia Rail is an imprint of
Crécy Publishing Limited
1a Ringway Trading Estate
Shadowmoss Road
Manchester M22 5LH

www.crecy.co.uk

Front Cover: Aldwych station was named Strand when it opened on 30 November 1907; its name was changed to Aldwych on 9 May 1915. The station and the branch from Holborn feeding it were closed on 30 September 1994 and since then the station has seen occasional use for filming and similar purposes. The name has also reverted to Strand! It is 25 September 2012. *John Glover*

Rear Cover Top: The north bank entrance shaft to the Tower Subway remains extant, albeit that it is a reconstruction of 1926. It is seen here on 4 June 2013. The inscription at the top reads: 'Constructed AD1868 London Hydraulic Power Company'. For taking passengers under the Thames, it contained a short-lived cable-hauled railway. *John Glover*

Rear Cover Bottom: Mark Lane opened in October 1884 to replace an earlier station and was renamed Tower Hill in 1946. The station reverted to its original location in 1967 when the 1884 station closed. The 1884 station's entrance was in Byward Street, seen here in 2013. *John Glover*

Contents Page: The District Railway built a typical station at Osterley & Spring Grove on the bridge over the line, with a station house alongside. It was closed on 24 March 1934 with the opening of the new Osterley station, about 350 yards further south, the next day. It is now a bookshop and is seen here on 27 May 2013. The bricked up arch that once lead to the footbridge and stairs to the platforms can be seen on the left of the building. The platforms are still in situ, albeit long disused. *John Glover*

BIBLIOGRAPHY

Bradshaw's Railway Guide; various reprints by David & Charles

By Tube Beyond Edgware; Tony Beard; 2002; Capital Transport Publishing

City and South London Railway, Re-opening December 1924; Reprint of booklet; 1990

Deep Tunnel Air Raid Shelters, London; Paper attributed to Halcrow's (project Consulting Engineers); 1942; may be found on www.subbrit.org.uk

London's Metropolitan Railway; Alan A Jackson; 1986; David & Charles

London's Secret Tubes; Andrew Emmerson & Tony Beard; 2nd edition, 2007; Capital Transport Publishing

London Underground, The – A Diagrammatic History; Douglas Rose; 6th edition; 2007

Northern Line Extensions, The, Underground No 9; Brian Hardy; 1981; London Underground Railway Society

Rails Through the Clay; D F Croome & A A Jackson; 2nd edition; 1993; Capital Transport Publishing

Railway Passenger Stations in England, Scotland and Wales – A Chronology; M E Quick; 3rd edition 2005; Railway & Canal Historical Society

West London Railway and the WLER, The; H V Borley & R W Kidner; 1981; The Oakwood Press.

See also Wikipedia on various topics and http://underground-history.co.uk

CONTENTS

Introduction

This book examines the stations on what became London Underground which, for one reason or another, are not or are no longer part of that railway. The main line railways generally are excluded, as are the station sites where there is effectively nothing left.

This book is about the positive views that can be had from open stations or from the street. When travelling on the deep tube lines, a rush of air may herald the site of a closed station, which with careful observation may be observed as a dark empty space, but the emphasis is on those works which can be seen properly.

Dates are given for reference purposes, though the published works do not always agree totally. A bibliography is provided, to which can be added the internet in general and Wikipedia in particular.

Throughout, the date quoted for station or other closures is that of the last train, often a Saturday, rather than the first day of 'no service' which was usually the following Monday. Imperial measures are used, as these seem to fit more satisfactorily into the largely historical nature of the subject.

John Glover
Worcester Park
Surrey
September 2013

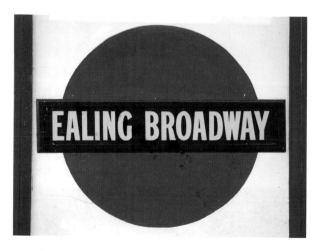

Curious survivors of times long past, Ealing Broadway District Line station still boasts a number of these signs. Despite their obvious age, it will be noted that the roundel formed a prominent feature of the design, even then. *John Glover*

The present King's Cross St Pancras Metropolitan, Circle and Hammersmith & City line platforms date from 1941. Before that they were a little further east. A small amount of the former eastbound platform can be observed where trains reach the daylight. At ground level, there is little more than a locked door in a wall, in a road known helpfully as King's Cross Bridge. It is 3 June 2013. *John Glover*

Of the four platforms at Willesden Green station, only the two in the centre, which form an island platform for the Jubilee Line, are used today. The outer ones are on the Metropolitan fast lines and have had no regular use since 1940. Nevertheless, the northbound Metropolitan platform still has a full range of buildings which date from the station's original opening on 24 November 1879. Out of sight behind these is the Great Central main line. The date is 8 June 2013. *John Glover*

Second thoughts: 1863-1935

FARRINGDON

In 1863 the Metropolitan Railway pioneered underground railways in the capital. The dimensions of its trains were akin to those of the main line railways, which in many ways they resembled. They just happened (for the most part) to be underground and built by what became known as the cut-and-cover method. This consisted of digging a large hole in the streets, securing the sides and providing a foundation and drainage for the track, and roofing in the whole.

The Metropolitan's very first line was from Paddington to Farringdon Street. This terminus was to be one of the shortest-lived stations, closing in 1865 so that the line could be extended to Moorgate. Nothing of it remains today.

A little later the District Railway (strictly but confusingly the Metropolitan District) joined in, with its lines rather nearer the River Thames.

TOWER SUBWAY

Or were there other construction methods? The builders of deep level tube railways had to find a viable alternative to steam traction, work out how ventilation was to be managed, and how passengers were to get between the platforms and the street.

The pioneering Tower Subway opened on 2 August 1870. A quarter of a mile long, it was built with the use of what, for its time, was a modern tunnelling shield. The route was beneath the river, where cut-and-cover was clearly impractical, rather than below the streets.

The dimensions were very tight, the tunnel being no more than 6ft 7¾in in diameter, but it did boast a diminutive railway of 2ft 6in gauge. The 'stations' at each end seem to have been no more than rudimentary platforms. Access was by steam-powered lifts at each end and there was a single car holding 12 (or perhaps 14) passengers. This was pulled by a rope fixed to a stationary engine for the first 100ft or so, after which it descended the incline under its own velocity and up the other side to the foot of the shaft.

Sadly it was not a success, the railway lasting less than four months. It became a pedestrian tunnel with the lifts replaced by stairs. It closed in 1898, shortly after the opening of Tower Bridge. But the Tower Subway's general method of construction provided useful lessons for what was to come.

Above: The Widened Lines were not physically separated from the main Underground route when this photograph was taken on 5 August 1976. This is the western end of Farringdon, with a pair of Class 105 Cravens DMUs from the Great Northern line heading towards Moorgate. Two London Underground 'A' stock trains in unpainted aluminium may be seen in the background. The nearside lines are now equipped with overhead electrification but the spur for the banking engine (for freight) has long since gone. *John Glover*

The north bank entrance shaft to the Tower Subway remains extant, albeit that it is a reconstruction of 1926. It is seen here on 4 June 2013. The inscription at the top reads: 'Constructed AD1868 London Hydraulic Power Company'. For taking passengers under the Thames, it contained a short -lived cable-hauled railway. *John Glover*

7

This plaque is on the sidewall of Regis House at 45 King William Street, on the north side of London Bridge. It is 1 June 2013. *John Glover*

KING WILLIAM STREET

The City & South London Railway (C&SLR) of 1890 was the first proper tube railway. Construction was by sinking shafts from the surface at suitable access points; some of these would later be used for lifts to the underground stations.

Following this, a shield was used to excavate the earth from the running tunnels for the trains and the larger diameter station tunnels. As the shield was pushed forward, the section thus excavated was lined immediately with cast iron segments. Originally, the trains were to be cable hauled, but this was later discarded in favour of electric locomotives.

The initial section ran from King William Street in the City, near the Monument, to Stockwell, with four intermediate stations at Borough, Elephant & Castle, Kennington and Oval. The line was 3¼ miles long. It was opened by the Prince of Wales, later King Edward VII, on 4 November 1890. Public services started on 18 December.

It too was built to restrictive dimensions, with a minimum running tunnel diameter of 10ft 2in. While small tunnels reduce the cost of construction, the limited dimensions later prevented the use of modern rolling stock working on the multiple-unit principle. This also reduces train weights and gives faster acceleration, allowing service frequencies to be enhanced.

King William Street was approached on sharp curves and originally there was one track with a platform each side (one for arriving, the other for departing passengers). In 1895 this was replaced by the more conventional two-tracked island arrangement.

System extension was a problem, in that the King William Street terminus, though in a good location, gave no opportunity for a northern line projection.

The upshot was that a line on a new alignment was constructed from a junction north of Borough station and carried under the river to London Bridge. From here it continued to Moorgate (1900), Angel (1901) and finally Euston (1907). To the south, Clapham Common was also reached in 1900.

King William Street terminus saw its last train on 24 February 1900. It thus lasted less than 10 years from opening, but both it and most of the disused tunnels from Borough would see subsequent wartime use.

On the surface, all that is to be seen today is a wall plaque.

BULL & BUSH

With few exceptions, the original tube railway network confined itself, with good reason, to the built up areas. Railways need patronage and this does not come from open country. One exception was the Hampstead tube, which took itself under Hampstead Heath to reach the open air amongst the turnip fields beside the Finchley Road. Here, this otherwise subterranean railway could find space for the car sheds it needed.

This matter-of-fact building is on the location of what might have been North End (or Bull & Bush) station. It is sited somewhat incongruously on Hampstead Way, a neighbourhood that might not have welcomed the presence of a fully-fledged Underground station. Apparently, this 1950s construction was designed to resemble an electricity substation. The date is 27 May 2013. *John Glover*

At Golders Green began the typical 20th century pattern of suburban development. The line opened throughout on 23 June 1907; in 1908 2.4m people used Golders Green station and by 1921 this figure had risen five-fold to 12.6m.

Such was the power of the Underground to stimulate house building and attract passengers and thus revenues. But it also had its downsides. A little nearer London, platform tunnels were constructed below Hampstead Heath in a location which was known officially as North End but more popularly as Bull & Bush after a nearby public house. (Time passes, and it is now The Old Bull & Bush.) This station would have been the deepest on the Underground network, 221ft below ground level.

Who, though, was going to use it? Proposals for nearby housing came to naught, and there was little else to generate traffic. The part-finished project was abandoned.

In the 1950s, a shaft was sunk to provide surface access to the platform area for civil defence purposes.

STATION (RE)NAMING

The next station south of Bull & Bush was Hampstead. Or was it? Originally to be named Heath Street, the name was changed to Hampstead before it was opened on 22 June 1907, but not before Heath Street appeared on the station wall tiles. They are still there today.

The former names of Hampstead (Heath End) on the Northern Line, Warren Street (Euston Road) also Northern Line, Marylebone (Great Central) Bakerloo Line and Arsenal (Gillespie Road) Piccadilly Line are still on show at the stations concerned. The names add an interesting comment on the past; all were photographed in 2013. *John Glover*

WARREN STREET

← Way out

WARR.

EUSTON · ROAD · L

NE

← Way out

MARYLEBONE

GREAT : CENTRAL

ARSENAL

 Way out →

ARSENAL

GILLESPIE : ROAD :

Other survivors are today's Arsenal which was Gillespie Road from its opening on 15 December 1906 to 31 October 1932, Marylebone was Great Central from 27 March 1907 until 15 April 1917, while Warren Street started life as Euston Road on 22 June 1907 and was renamed on 7 June 1908.

Similar tiling patterns survive at many other stations, which retain their original names.

HOUNSLOW CENTRAL

The District Railway had a number of western branches. Until 1964, one of these was to Hounslow West, via Northfields.

West of Acton Town, the District proceeded to Osterley and then south to a terminus at Hounslow Town. The line was opened on 1 May 1883. This was in a never fulfilled hope of being able to extend into London & South Western Railway territory. The following year, on 21 July 1884, junction completion enabled District trains to take a new westerly line to Hounslow West. (Present day names are used, but three of the four Hounslow stations have had other names during their existence.)

All services to the Hounslow Town terminus were withdrawn on 31 March 1886 and Hounslow Central opened the following day. But that too was later deemed unsatisfactory; Hounslow Town was reopened on I March 1903 and a new spur constructed. From 13 June 1905 this enabled what were now electric trains to reverse at Hounslow Town and then continue via Hounslow Central to Hounslow West. The direct route omitting Hounslow Town was closed instead.

This new arrangement didn't work well, either. A new Hounslow East station on the direct route to Hounslow West was opened on 2 May 1909, with both routes to Hounslow Town and the station itself closing the day before. Its site is now hidden under Hounslow bus station. Since then, all services have operated via the present route to Hounslow West.

Piccadilly Line trains were introduced from 1933, running in parallel with District services. The latter ceased in 1964.

Further changes in 1975 are discussed subsequently (see page 47).

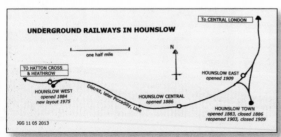

Underground Railways in Hounslow.

That Hounslow Town station found itself on a branch that failed to be extended was never going to count in its favour. This plaque on the railings outside what is now a bus station notes the main events. It was photographed on 27 May 2013. *John Glover*

LONDON BOROUGH OF HOUNSLOW

Hounslow Town Centre Project

Local History

Hounslow Town Railway Station

Hounslow was a busy place during the Coaching Age. But the era of coach-horses had ended by the time the Metropolitan and District Railway reached this part of West London in 1883.

An imposing terminus station once stood on the site of the present bus garage. However, plans to continue the line southwards to Twickenham were abandoned and the Railway was extended westwards instead. As a result, Hounslow East Station soon replaced the Broadway Terminus.

Hounslow Town Station, in use between 1883-1886 and 1905-1909.

When London General Omnibus took over the site of Hounslow Town Station in 1912, the White Bear public house which also stood there quickly followed its neighbour, the railway station, to a new home on Kingsley Road.

Once steam-hauled trains on the Metropolitan District line were electrified in 1905. The route was attached to the Piccadilly Underground railway and came under the control of London Transport in 1933.

This is the site of the former Hounslow Town station, now bus station and garage as seen on 27 May 2013 from what would have been the buffer stop end. This is about 250yd from the present Hounslow East station. *John Glover*

The remains of City Road station at street level consist of this ventilation shaft, standing in splendid isolation. It is seen here on 1 June 2013. *John Glover*

CITY ROAD

While the extensions to the C&SLR were built to slightly larger tunnel gauges to those adopted originally, it was all still some way short of what became the Underground standard of 11ft 8½in. Eventually, it was agreed to carry out a whole series of works; these consisted of extension south to Morden, north beyond Euston to Camden Town where it would join the 'Hampstead tube', together with linking the southern end of that line from the present Charing Cross to Kennington. These works were completed between 1924 and 1926 and the essential features of what is now the Northern Line were put in place.

Station works generally included platform lengthening to accommodate longer trains, the provision of escalators at some (with the associated mismatch between the upper and lower landings when compared with lifts), retiling throughout and attention to the surface buildings.

But such work is extremely costly; was it always justified? The answer for City Road station, between Angel and Old Street, turned out to be no. That station was closed, unmodified, after its last train on 8 August 1922.

SOUTH KENTISH TOWN

Inevitably, some station investments proved more worthwhile than others. South Kentish Town, between Kentish Town and Camden Town, had modest usage.

The end came in unusual and perhaps unique circumstances. A strike by staff at Lots Road Power Station caused this station (like several others) to be shut on the afternoon of 5 June 1924. Management took advantage of the situation and decided that closure should be permanent — and that was it!

The station building is now commercial premises.

PICCADILLY CLOSURES

The northern terminus of the Piccadilly was at Finsbury Park, and a long-standing agreement with the Great Northern Railway and its successors had prevented further expansion. But if that happened, journey times would be tiresomely long due to the number of intermediate stops. Could some be omitted?

Three closures resulted. The last trains called at Down Street (between Green Park and Hyde Park Corner) on 21 May 1932, at York Road (between King's Cross and Caledonian Road) on 17 September 1932, and at Brompton Road (between Knightsbridge and South Kensington) on 29 July 1934.

It might be mentioned here that Dover Street station, which seemingly disappeared in 1933, was reincarnated as Green Park.

The surface buildings of these and South Kentish Town, such as they remain, are unmistakably the handiwork of Leslie Green. He was the company architect and known for his steel framed station buildings, the frontages of which sported 'ox-blood' coloured tiles. Another Leslie Green disused surface building may be found at the former Euston Northern Line entrance in Drummond Street.

Right: Down Street Piccadilly Line station was in a side road of that name. The platforms are still accessible from the surface, via the firmly closed door to the left. The rest of the surface building, seen here on 27 May 2013, is given over to commercial uses. *John Glover*

Below: Seen here on 3 June 2013, York Road Piccadilly Line station is surprisingly complete given that by then it had been closed to passengers for over 70 years. *John Glover*

Brompton Road Piccadilly Line station was situated off the Brompton Road in Cottage Place. That part of the building that remains still declares its origins on 27 May 2013. *John Glover*

HYDE PARK CORNER

Another reason for change was the introduction of subsurface ticket halls reached by more than one set of stairs from the street. That rendered the surface buildings largely superfluous. One to suffer such fate was Hyde Park Corner station; the original building in Knightsbridge is now a restaurant.

BRITISH MUSEUM 1933

A series of works concerned interchanges between lines. If built by separate companies without a common interest, the concept of passenger interchange does not rate highly.

At Holborn, the Central Line of 1900 crossed over the Piccadilly of 1906, but the stations of each were some distance apart. The outcome was that the Central's British Museum station was closed and new platforms were created further east at the Piccadilly's Holborn. Direct interchange thus became available between the lines concerned in 1933.

The last trains called at British Museum on 24 September of that year. Military use was made of the premises for a time, but the surface buildings were later totally demolished. The site is now occupied by the offices of the Nationwide Building Society.

THE BRILL BRANCH

The metals of the Metropolitan Railway extended far beyond what at any time might have been defined as urban London. Brill was recorded as 50¼ miles from London, while Verney Junction was shown as a quarter mile further. They were both as distant as Brighton.

The original District Railway station of South Harrow, between Sudbury Hill and Rayners Lane, was opened on 28 June 1903. It was decided that it could with advantage be relocated a little to the north, and the new station, with a new entrance, opened on 4 July 1935. The 1903 buildings on the eastern side of the line remain and are in use for London Underground staff. They are just beyond the present platform ends. This view was taken on 26 April 2008. *John Glover*

Hyde Park Corner station is still very much open, but now accessible only by subway. The original station building, seen here on 27 May 2013, is now a restaurant. The additions will be noticed. *John Glover*

The Metropolitan was a real railway, in the sense that it was much more than a Metro system. Thus it carried goods traffic as well as passenger, while its whole operation was more reminiscent of a main-line undertaking.

That its ambitions should take it so far from London was the wish to link with what became the Great Central Railway in its bid to create the last main line into London (Marylebone). That was achieved in 1899. This came from the drive of the Chairman of both undertakings, (Sir) Edward Watkin, who hoped that one day there would be a railway from Manchester to Paris, all under his control.

That takes the story to Quainton Road, itself 44½ miles distant, where the Wotton Tramway, or the Brill branch, diverged from the main line. This was built by the Duke of Buckingham as a private railway for his estate purposes, but came into Metropolitan hands from 1 December 1899.

This was mostly a roadside tramway running the seven miles from Quainton Road to Brill. Traffic by any standards was modest, and when the Metropolitan came into the hands of the London Passenger Transport Board on 1 July 1933 it seemed unlikely that it would last for long.

So it turned out, and the tramway closed on 30 November 1935. The 1910 timetable shown comes from Bradshaw; it changed little up to closure, save for the abandonment of Sunday operations.

The Board's Annual Report for the year ended 30 June 1936 recorded the event as follows:

'The train services provided on the Brill Branch have resulted in a loss of roundly £4,000 per annum. The traffic was exceedingly light, the total number of passenger journeys in the year being 18,000, or fewer than 50 a day. The annual goods and mineral traffic amounted to some 7,600 tons only, representing about 20 tons a day. There has been no development in the traffic, and as, owing to its volume, it seemed quite feasible for it to be dealt with by road means of conveyance, the Board took steps to give notice for the closing of this branch line, and such notice having expired, it was closed on 30 November 1935.'

On a lightly laid line like this, negligible railway assets remain more than 75 years after its demise.

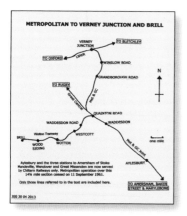

VERNEY JUNCTION

Seven months after the Brill closure, it was the turn of the line between Quainton Road and Verney Junction. This, the former Aylesbury & Buckingham Railway, was closed on 4 July 1936. Both the end stations remained open for the time being for the sparse services operated by the main lines. The intermediate stations of Winslow

Left: Metropolitan to Verney Junction and Brill.

Below: Brill branch timetable, *Bradshaw's Guide*, August 1910.

		Week Days.					Sundays.					Week Days.					Sndys
Miles		mrn	aft	aft	aft	aft		mrn	aft		Miles		mrn	mrn	aft	aft	aft	mrn	aft
	QuaintonRd.dp	9 36	12 54	0 6	42	9 20	....	11 21	6 30	...		Brill ......dep.	8 20	10 34	3 7	5 30	8 30	7 05 35
1½	Waddesdon	9 45	12 14	4	8 6 50	9 28	....	11 29	6 38	....	1½	Wood Siding ...	Sig.	Sig.	Sig.	Sig.	Sig.	Sig. Sig.
1¾	Westcott	Sig.	8ig.	8ig.	8ig.	Sig.	....	8ig.	8ig.	....	2½	Wotton	8 40	10 51	3 24	5 48	8 47	7 18 53
3½	Wotton	9 58	12 27	4 21	7 3	9 41	....	11 42	6 51	....	4½	Westcott	Sig.	8ig.	Sig.	Sig.	Sig.	Sig. Sig.
5	Wood Siding ..	8ig.	8ig.	8ig.	8ig.	Sig.	....	11 42	8ig.	....	5	Waddesdon ..	8 52	11 3	3 36	6	8 59	7 30 6
6½	Brill .... arr.	10 14	12 45	4 37	7 19	9 57	....	11 58	7 9	....	6½	QuaintnRd.	396	9 0	11 13	44 6 10	9 7	7 40 6 18

Sig., for signal, indicates that the train stops only on request.

Road and Granborough Road were closed completely, as was Waddesdon station between Quainton Road and Aylesbury.

In the timetable operational from 30 September 1935, less than a year before closure, there were eight trains in each direction between Quainton Road and Verney Junction. Of these, only two were operated by London Transport, the rest by the London & North Eastern Railway. By now, no trains ran on Sundays.

Most were through services to at least Aylesbury; one that wasn't was the 8.10am service from Quainton Road to Liverpool Street via Baker Street, operated by London Transport. This train carried a Pullman Car. The LNER provided a branch connection from Verney Junction.

Reduced to single track, the former main line through Quainton Road still carries modest amounts of freight. This station was last used by Metropolitan trains on 29 May 1948 and by British Railways trains on 2 March 1963. It is still served occasionally by a diesel unit linking the Buckinghamshire Railway Centre, located here, with Aylesbury.

Nothing of any consequence remains of the intermediate stations on the branch, but Verney Junction still boasts disused platforms and a single track, albeit out of use, on the line between Oxford and Bletchley. It is intended that this will become part of a double track electrified and mainly freight route from Southampton to the Midland Main Line, the *Electric Spine*.

The location of Verney Junction station is remarkably remote; there are only a handful of residential properties in the vicinity. This 1994 view was taken from the western end of the former station on the line from Oxford and looking east towards Bletchley. The Metropolitan platform was at the far end, on the right hand side. Only the station house remains. *John Glover*

Quainton Road station, which as its name suggests is not very close to Quainton village, was photographed on 12 April 1998. The station is still in occasional use, albeit now with only one main line track passing through. The rest of the premises are part of the Buckingham Railway Centre. The former platform for Brill still exists, and may just be seen on the right. *John Glover*

New Works Programme from 1935

There was clearly much more to do, the result of which was the extensive New Works Programme, 1935-40. Much of this was completed, albeit often a little later than planned. The discussion here though is concerned with the stations that were closed as a result.

BAKERLOO TO FINCHLEY ROAD

Dealing satisfactorily with the growth of traffic on the Metropolitan had been assisted by the quadrupling from Wembley Park to Finchley Road, but that had only a limited effect on the bottleneck of the two-tracked section in tunnel thence to Baker Street.

A new junction for the Bakerloo was built at Baker Street, with an extension to Finchley Road. Here it took over the two centre tracks to Wembley Park and thence by the Metropolitan to Stanmore, opened in 1932.

The Bakerloo was to provide the all-stations local service, with Metropolitan trains from Baker Street stopping only at Finchley Road and then Wembley Park, or sometimes first stop Harrow-on-the-Hill.

The existing Metropolitan line stations at Lord's (of which nothing remains at street level), Marlborough Road (road now renamed Marlborough Place), and Swiss Cottage were closed. A Bakerloo replacement was built at St John's Wood, while Swiss Cottage was in effect an adaptation of the previous Metropolitan station. There are no surface buildings here.

The new Bakerloo stations (and line) were opened on 20 November 1939; that included the entire operation of the Stanmore branch. The whole became part of the Jubilee Line on 1 May 1979.

ST MARY'S

Between Whitechapel and Aldgate East, St Mary's was effectively redundant after the latter was rebuilt. This had resulted in the Aldgate East platforms being moved nearer Whitechapel and a second entrance being provided at that end of the station. It closed on 30 April 1938 and was later largely destroyed by bombing.

NORTHERN HEIGHTS

The biggest planned investment of the New Works was known as the Northern Heights. It was an ambitious undertaking, but much of it was never completed. It is discussed here in detail.

The extension of what was then the Bakerloo Line from Baker Street to Finchley Road and beyond rendered the three stations on the parallel Metropolitan Line redundant. Marlborough Road, a little to the north of the present St John's Wood Jubilee Line station, survives. It was photographed on 27 May 2013 in a gleaming white finish, though it appears to have neither a current tenant nor use. *John Glover*

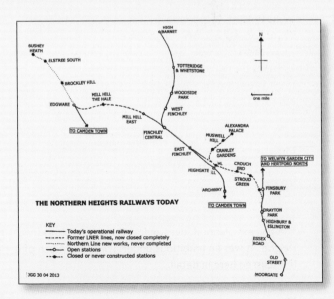

The Northern Heights railways today.

The two central platforms at East Finchley, photographed on 27 May 2013, are used only by trains proceeding to or from Highgate depot, which is just about visible in the distance. All other passenger services use the outside tracks; a train is seen about to disappear into the 17-mile tunnel to Morden, having already crossed the bridge over the Great North Road. How different things here might have been! *John Glover*

Mill Hill East was destined for greater things than the terminus of a shuttle service from Finchley Central, to which it is also linked by a local bus route of similar frequency. This is the view looking towards Edgware on 3 June 2013. To the left would have been the second track and an additional platform; as can be seen, the route beyond this station is firmly blocked. *John Glover*

Edgware was to have had additional tracks and platforms for the Bushey Heath extension in the area now occupied by the miscellany of buildings seen here on 3 June 2013. In the end, the station retains two platforms under the overall roof (left), with a third platform completely devoid of any shelter for passengers (right). The air of uncompleted business remains. *John Glover*

Even the destination plates for the aborted Northern Heights scheme were manufactured. Services would have been provided by the 1938 stock, a Driving Motor Car of which is seen here. It is resident in the London Transport Museum. *John Glover*

On the Great Northern line out of King's Cross, the London & North Eastern Railway had a problem. Put simply, this was passenger demand for more trains than could be accommodated. At Finsbury Park where all the suburban services came together, many feet were regularly trampled by passengers making quick changes between trains.

Meanwhile, London Transport had the Great Northern & City end-to-end service running the 3½ miles between Moorgate and Finsbury Park with four intermediate stations. Ever since opening in 1904 there had been ambitions to extend over the Great Northern network, but without result.

Fortuitously perhaps in view of later events, this line was built to main line dimensions and with long platforms, though neither was ever exploited by London Transport.

THE PROPOSALS

London Transport's New Works Programme provided a possible solution to the problems of both parties. The idea was to bring the trains from Moorgate in the deep cutting at Drayton Park station to the surface. From here, they would run alongside the LNER services on the eastern side to Finsbury Park station, using new platforms and with new bridges for the road crossings.

They would then bridge the East Coast main line, joining the branch that would take them to Edgware (11¼ miles from King's Cross), High Barnet (also 11¼ miles) and Alexandra Palace (6¾ miles).

The station house at Stroud Green is all that remains. This view was taken on 3 June 2013 from the site of the former wooden platforms on the railway bridge, but of these nothing remains. The railway right of way now forms a pleasant Parkland Walk from Highgate (exc) to Finsbury Park (exc). *John Glover*

The hands of London Transport are clearly visible in this view of the intermediate station of Crouch End on the Northern Heights development. The platforms have been rebuilt and lengthened and some work has been done on the station buildings, but all to no avail. It is 10 April 2005. *John Glover*

This general view of what would have been Highgate High Level station shows that much remains intact 60 years after the last passenger train departed. Looking west, the former station buildings (still occupied) are in the foreground, with the 'new' island platform in the centre. Access to this was via steps to the lower level ticket hall, which itself remains in use. The roundel on the far side marks another station entrance. It is 27 May 2013. *John Glover*

In this view of the east side entrance to Highgate station, the former island platform and other buildings can be seen on 27 May 2013. The construction to the right houses the up (only) escalator from the ticket hall to the Archway Road. The station is in a deep cutting, which accounts for the unusual arrangement of tunnels (not shown) at both ends of the High Level station. *John Glover*

The terminus of the branch to Alexandra Palace was to serve the Palace itself, and nothing else. On closure of the branch in 1954, the ticket office (left) survived. It now houses CUFOS (Community Use For Old Station) and was photographed on 3 June 2013. This view looks north-east along the site of the former platform and trackbed. The Palace is on the right. *John Glover*

Coincidentally, the Northern Line Underground would be extended from Archway to Highgate and East Finchley, joining the LNER at a rebuilt and extended station. Finchley Central would have had its three platforms extended to four. What is now the Mill Hill East branch would be double tracked, and on reaching Edgware this would join the existing Northern Line route of 1924. The LNER Edgware passenger station would be abandoned.

The combined railway would then be extended a further 2¾ miles on new construction to Brockley Hill, Elstree South and Bushey Heath.

All lines mentioned would be electrified on the fourth-rail system and operated by London Transport. This would be a surface railway, apart from the section south of Drayton Park, the two short Highgate tunnels and a new one to be built at Elstree.

In late 1938, it was anticipated that all would be in operation by December 1940.

THE REALITY

The first signs were encouraging. The tunnels were dug north from Archway, coming to the surface just short of East Finchley station, and electric trains reached High Barnet in 1940. Mill Hill East was added to the network in 1941 to serve the nearby Inglis Barracks, but the demands of war meant that there matters stopped.

Although quite a lot of electrification work had by then been done in the preparation of the LNER branches, it was never resumed. General shortages of labour and materials in post-war Britain, to say nothing of government funds, were severe constraints. To this had to be added the Green Belt legislation. If the scope for new house building north of Edgware was to be much curtailed, there was little point in building a new railway to serve it.

WITHDRAWAL

The end was prolonged. What was by now British Railways continued to operate the Alexandra Palace service. This was done with some reluctance, since during the coal and manpower shortages of 1951-52 services on the entire branch from Finsbury Park via Stroud Green, Crouch End, Highgate, Cranley Gardens and Muswell Hill were withdrawn for a couple of months. Final and permanent withdrawal came on 3 July 1954.

Steam services to East Finchley had already ceased. Further work on the extensions north of Edgware was in abeyance, followed by formal abandonment.

British Railways continued to serve the goods yards at the former LNER stations, the last of these ceasing in 1964. At Finchley Central the road collection and delivery (C&D) service remained active for many years.

A residual traffic was the periodic Underground stock transfer between Drayton Park and Neasden via Stroud Green. Haulage was by LT battery locomotives. These workings ceased on 6 October 1970.

The underground platforms on the former Great Northern & City line tend to be cavernous and even mildly eerie when there are few people around. This is the Moorgate terminus in April 1986, with No 313.024 soon to depart. *John Glover*

Essex Road was part of the Great Northern & City Railway, which later fell under the ownership of the Metropolitan Railway. It thus became part of London Transport, by whom it was last served on 3 October 1975. The present operator is First Capital Connect. A curious feature of this modestly used station is that passengers descend by lift from the street to a lower landing, from which it is then necessary to climb 30 steps to reach platform level. This view was taken on 4 June 2013. *John Glover*

LATER DEVELOPMENTS

The construction of the Victoria Line came in the 1960s; this used the terminal platforms of the Moorgate services at Finsbury Park. Operations of the latter were cut back from 3 October 1964 to Drayton Park only. The east side of the platform at Finsbury Park was used by the southbound Victoria Line, the west side for the westbound Piccadilly.

At Drayton Park, the GN&C line comes to the surface and pantographs are raised. A Class 313 unit in Network SouthEast livery is departing towards Finsbury Park on 6 April 1998. The running of through trains from Moorgate to the Great Northern had long been anticipated, but few could have imagined that it would take over 70 years to achieve. *John Glover*

The second development was connection to the National Rail (then British Rail) system. If the Underground's Moorgate shuttle was not to become part of an extended Northern Line, then it could be joined to the Great Northern inner-suburban services. This had the additional benefit of freeing up King's Cross station platforms; if passengers wanted to travel to the West End rather than the City, the Victoria Line (fully opened 1971) would offer them a cross-platform change at Highbury & Islington. New tunnelling took place here to enable this to happen.

The remainder of the line was closed in 1975 marking the end of Underground interests. London Underground remains the station operator at Moorgate, Old Street and Highbury & Islington.

Although the Great Northern main line was electrified at 25kV ac overhead, the section south of Drayton Park is operated at 750v dc third rail due to restricted tunnel clearances. During the station stop at Drayton Park, the pantograph is lowered (or raised) by the driver before proceeding.

The line was reopened as part of British Railways on 16 August 1976 (8 November for Old Street to Moorgate), with services to Welwyn Garden City and to Hertford North. There were no station closures, only changes in use.

PRESENT SITUATION

More recently, weekend and late evening Great Northern services have been diverted to King's Cross, when patronage to the City is very light.

On the Northern Line proper, Mill Hill East services are now usually provided by a shuttle from Finchley Central.

To summarise, the aspirations of the Northern Heights scheme were largely negated by World War 2 and its aftermath, though the much later Great Northern electrification scheme rescued that part of the Underground from a somnolent existence.

Was the failure to complete the investment programme to operate from Moorgate to Bushey Heath via Finchley Central, or to Alexandra Palace, a mistake? For the former, it is difficult to see how sufficient traffic could ever have been generated, while the Ally Pally branch, curving round as it did to terminate at the back of the Palace, took a far from direct route. One can regret the wasted preparation work, but it is difficult to conclude other than that the whole would have been a sizeable drain on the Underground's resources, with only modest user benefits.

Overall, there were 25 stations involved in the Northern Heights scheme. The table summarises their fate:

Northern Heights stations

Station(s)	Total	What happened?
Moorgate to Drayton Park	5	In 1976 became part of what is now a completely separate national railway operation
Finsbury Park	1	New platforms never built
Stroud Green to Alexandra Palace	6	Adapted to varying extents but all closed on 3 July 1954, never served by the Underground
Highgate Low Level	1	Built new, operational 1941
East Finchley	1	Comprehensively rebuilt and operational 1939
Finchley Central to High Barnet	5	Adapted for Underground role, but few works actually carried out. Operational 1940
Mill Hill East	1	Operational 1941 at end of single track branch
Mill Hill (The Hale)	1	Closed 9 September 1939, never served by the Underground
Edgware (LNER)	–	Not part of scheme, closed 9 September 1939
Edgware (LT)	1	Partially adapted, but still serves only the line towards Golders Green
Brockley Hill to Bushey Heath	3	Never built

WHITE CITY — CENTRAL LINE

The New Works Programme saw long extensions proposed for the Central Line, but the reconstruction described here had its origins many years before.

Two large-scale exhibitions were scheduled for White City in 1908; these were the Franco-British Exhibition and the Summer Olympics. In order to help cope with the large numbers expected to attend, changes were made to the Shepherd's Bush terminus of the Central London Railway (CLR). These are shown on the accompanying map.

The new arrangements saw trains leaving Shepherd's Bush station on the westbound track, which curved sharply to the north and over the eastbound track. They then started an anti-clockwise movement on a tight radius curve.

Trains called at the new Wood Lane station platforms (one for alighting and one for joining passengers) on each side of the single track, before continuing on the eastbound line back to Shepherd's Bush and thence to Bank.

This convoluted arrangement also had to allow for trains to access the depot, for which a reversing movement was necessary. Nearly all of these movements took place underground, but it was the only time the original CLR reached the open air at all.

The new station platforms at Wood Lane were opened on 14 May 1908. Given what was later likely to be only spasmodic use, it was intended that they should be closed after the exhibitions.

Next though was the westward extension of the line to Ealing Broadway in conjunction with the Great Western. The opening took place on 3 August 1920. A new track for westbound trains was laid from the outer side of the loop before reaching the station to take trains towards Ealing, and the second track from Ealing joined the outer side of the loop on the far side of the station platforms.

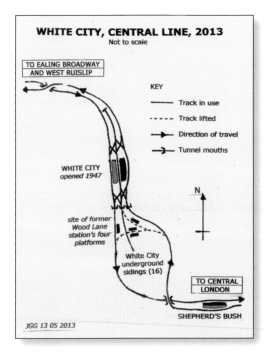

White City, Central Line, 2013.

Both these extensions were provided with a single platform so that non-terminating trains could also call.

Matters were thus much improved, but it was the building of the additional Central Line branch to West Ruislip which produced the opportunity to close Wood Lane altogether. This saw the construction of the new White City station, beyond this whole area and above ground. It was opened on 23 November 1947, together with the rest of the line to West Ruislip. Wood Lane closed permanently on the previous day.

White City station has a curious back-to-front feel, as the continued use of the former terminal loop means trains run on the right rather than the left of the two tracks. A flyover further west restores the normal situation.

The remains of the unusual Wood Lane have now disappeared completely as a result of the Westfield shopping development.

Today's White City station, seen here on 11 July 2007 has an eastbound train of 1992 stock which will shortly depart towards the camera (and tunnel mouth) on the left, while westbound trains on the right proceed away from the camera. The centre track with platforms both sides is used for terminating services. *John Glover*

War and the pretend stations

This chapter is concerned mainly with the deep level underground shelters provided in central London, but considers also effects on station closures.

UXBRIDGE ROAD

Little remembered today, the construction of what is now the Hammersmith & City Line included a short spur from the west of the present Latimer Road station to the West London Line. This was at the behest of the Great Western Railway, which saw it as a means to access Kensington.

Services from Farringdon Street (the original Metropolitan terminus) had commenced on 1 July 1864 and terminated at what is now Kensington Olympia.

A new station was built at Uxbridge Road, immediately to the north of today's Holland Park gyratory. This was opened for Metropolitan traffic on 1 November 1869.

The line was electrified on the fourth-rail system on 3 December 1906 and was worked as a joint Great Western and Metropolitan Railway venture.

Bradshaw records that in 1910 the services from Aldgate to Kensington Olympia ran about every 20min, taking 35min or so for the journey. By 1922 the eastern terminus had become Edgware Road and the Sunday service had been discontinued, but the service pattern remained similar.

Severe bomb damage in 1940 meant that the last Underground trains ran on 19 October. They were never restored. The Latimer Road curve was removed, Uxbridge Road station was demolished and all traces of it gradually disappeared.

Surprisingly, that was not the end. The resuscitation of the West London Line, its electrification and the introduction of local services by London Overground and the Southern Train Operating Company resulted in the building of a new two platformed and staffed station on virtually the same site. This opened for traffic on 28 September 2008.

There was one big change, in that it is now called Shepherd's Bush. It is situated adjacent to the re-sited Central Line Underground station entrance and both are close to the new bus station.

AIR RAIDS

The safest place in war during an air raid is likely to be in a deep level underground station. Or so it seemed to many Londoners and this was acknowledged by authority. Although initially it was intended to keep stations free from such visitors, the demand was not resisted for long.

Uxbridge Road station on the West London Line and used by the Underground was closed in 1940. The station was reincarnated on 28 September 2008 as Shepherd's Bush station, on virtually the same site. It is placed opposite the revamped entrance to London Underground's Central Line station of the same name. The date is 22 October 2008. *John Glover*

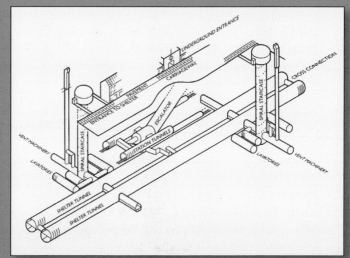

This plan shows the general arrangements common to the deep level shelters, with their two entrances and their relationship with the existing Underground station.

The northern entrance of the Belsize Park shelter is now incorporated in the leafy enclave of a private housing estate off Haverstock Hill. The main structure with its circular drum, the ventilation shaft and ancillary buildings are all visible here. It is 3 June 2013. *John Glover*

Most of these stations are still there today and so outside the present subject matter. One that was not was the former C&SLR line north from Borough to where it was blocked on reaching the Thames.

Another approach was purpose designed and built deep level shelters. There were, eventually, eight of these, all but one below Northern Line stations. The idea dated from pre-war discussions on how to relieve the pressure of numbers on the Underground system. Were newly constructed deep level tubes an answer? The trains would have limited stopping patterns, with lesser used stations bypassed.

The seven Northern Line stations where shelter construction was carried out were Belsize Park, Camden Town, Goodge Street, Stockwell, Clapham North, Clapham Common and Clapham South.

THE SHELTERS

All shelters were to be of a uniform design, subject to site constraints and located at existing tube stations. The internal diameter of these tunnels was to be 16ft 6in, similar to those of the Great Northern & City line, which today carries full sized trains. This may be compared with the 12ft diameter or thereabouts for the tube system at that time. It was intended that they could eventually form running tunnels rather than stations on a new deep level line.

The tunnels were also to be very long; at 1,200ft, this was equivalent to about 23 cars of the 1938 tube stock then operating on the Northern Line. Some were extended to 1,300ft, or even 1,400ft.

Tunnels of these dimensions were going to be very capacious and 9,600 persons per shelter was the original planned capacity, later scaled back to 8,000. Even so, this was a very considerable number, given that the facilities provided needed to match.

In each of the main shelter tunnels, a floor was inserted at mid-height, with another near the bottom. Separate accommodation was thus was available at two levels. For sleeping, bunks were arranged crossways on one side of the gangway (in three tiers) and longitudinally on the other. Bunks were 2ft wide, with the same vertical distance between them.

VENTILATION

Some of the problems were common to the tube system. Thus those using the shelters needed to be provided with fresh air, to include the extraction of vitiated air using fans and specially constructed shafts to the surface. Sanitation was another requirement, given also that the shelters were below mains sewers. Compressed air was used to force the waste up to sewer level.

Water and sewage storage tanks were also installed.

Medical aid posts were needed, as was warden accommodation. Canteens were a must; these were 40ft long, with eight provided in each shelter. Such was the quantity of food needed that small lifts were installed in the surface access shafts.

These ancillary services were located adjacent to the cross passages which linked the main tunnels, themselves at two levels.

Lighting also needed special attention, ranging from full lighting, quarter or emergency lighting, or dimmed lighting while the shelterers slept.

Construction was under the aegis of Government, with London Transport as their agents. Building started in 1940 and all were completed during 1942.

ACCESS

The whole was built using two working shafts that, on completion, become access points. All the deep level shelters were built below the existing stations carrying the same name; direct staircase access from the platforms or passageways was also possible.

It was always intended that general public access would be by spiral staircases from the two surface entrances. These were double spirals, so that the occupants of each floor could proceed rapidly to their own shelter places. The stairs ended above ground level, to prevent tunnel flooding from burst water mains, and were protected from bombing by heavily reinforced concrete pillboxes.

Two entrances accommodated the sheer numbers of people involved and the time this could take, but also as an insurance against either being damaged by bombing.

'The Drum' was the southern entrance to the Clapham South deep level shelter and it has now been sensitively incorporated into an apartment block completed in 2012. Since the war, it has been used as troop billets in 1946, as hotel accommodation during the Festival of Britain in 1951 and for Coronation visitors in 1953. It was also used as a temporary home for the first immigrants from the Caribbean, who arrived on MV *Empire Windrush* in June 1948. It is seen here on 3 June 2013. *John Glover*

The northern deep level shelter entrance to that at Clapham Common can be seen from Carpenter's Place, off Clapham High Street. This consists of the familiar circular 'pillbox' with a square brick ventilation intake on the roof. There are brick extensions at both ends and a separate ventilation shaft to the left. The date is 3 June 2013. *John Glover*

The centre of a busy traffic gyratory seems an unlikely location for the entrance to an air raid shelter for the masses, but wartime conditions were very different. This is the northern entrance at Stockwell, seen here on 3 June 2013. In 1999, the outside of the Rotunda, as is in known, was decorated with a mural by local artist Brian Barnes with the assistance of students from Stockwell Park School. *John Glover*

The ungainly northern entrance to one of these shelters may be seen to advantage at Camden Town. It is 27 May 2013. Everything here is brick, or brick faced, and unpainted. The circular 'pillbox' has the ventilation shaft on the roof and there are brick extensions on either side. One wonders what the key Underground architect of that period, Charles Holden, made of them. *John Glover*

Fresh air supplies had to guard against a possible gas attack and dust from bombed buildings.

The unlovely surface constructions were positioned at roundly the one quarter and three quarter points in the length of the shelter tunnels. Each consists of a circular pillbox and a small brick building on a metal framework around an open shaft.

They remain in situ.

USAGE

Five were opened as public shelters (as opposed to government or military use), but not as it turned out until 1944. From 1943, the Goodge Street shelter became General Eisenhower's London headquarters.

After the war the shelters were used variously, perhaps for temporary accommodation, or the storage of papers and manuscripts. The storage use continues in some cases; others have in effect been abandoned.

None was ever used by an operational railway.

The Eisenhower Centre in Chenies Road near Goodge Street station is one of the more prominent of these installations. This building consists of two large concrete blocks joined. The circular one on the left has a ventilation shaft above it; the other is octagonal in shape. The entrance is at the front. It is the more southerly of the two surface buildings here. This picture was taken on 27 March 2013. *John Glover*

'Chancery Station House' is the name above the door of the former station entrance to Chancery Lane Central Line. The station is now reached by steps down from the pavement a little further to the east. This building in High Holborn became an entrance to the deep level wartime shelter and a firmly locked door can be seen to the left of the main entrance. It is 1 June 2013. *John Glover*

CHANCERY LANE

That left Chancery Lane on the Central Line. Here the Central London Railway surface buildings had been made redundant by the building of a low-level ticket office with access to the platforms by escalators in the 1930s. Entrance from the street was by stairs on the street corners.

The original station entrance with the distinctive architecture of Harry Bell Measures (pinkish terracotta with red brick) survives as commercial premises on High Holborn. It was available for use as access to another deep level shelter.

This was used as a communications centre and post-war as Holborn telephone exchange.

The partly finished Central Line extension workings were also put to wartime use and the completed tunnels from Leytonstone (exclusive) to Newbury Park (exclusive) did service as an underground factory for the Plessey company. Access routes included the future stations.

Buckhurst Hill was one of the ex-Great Eastern Railway stations acquired by the Underground as part of the Central Line extensions. At the London end of the station can be seen the former station house and remains of the staggered platform which existed from opening in 1856 to reconstruction in 1892. The date is 4 June 2013. *John Glover*

Later 20th Century: 1950-1999

Post war meant recovery, and for the Underground further progress was noticeable by its absence. Later, it began to be seen more as an asset to be exploited rather than an urban problem.

SOUTH ACTON

The 1,232yd branch from Acton Town to South Acton, with no intermediate stations, was opened to passenger traffic on 13 June 1905. In the early days there were occasional through services to Hounslow West, but in 1932 the branch was reduced to single track and operated as a shuttle. The two car trains were marked at one end 'Acton Town Non Stop' and at the other 'South Acton All Stations'.

By the outbreak of war the shuttle was provided by a double-ended single car.

The track at the District station at South Acton was at a level a little above that of the adjacent but separate North London Line station. The basic station building featured a small ticket office. A passage linked the two.

Such was the length of the line that one train could provide a service every four minutes. This gave rise to the erroneous popular belief that the schedule was based on tea-making activities at Acton Town (there and back while the kettle boils).

The branch did afford a connection into and out of British Railways' North London Line services, but the economics were against it. The last trains ran on 28 February 1959 and very little remains.

GLOUCESTER ROAD & SOUTH KENSINGTON

The use of Gloucester Road and South Kensington stations by both the Metropolitan and District companies resulted in the duplication of facilities to the extent that four tracks were provided where two might have been adequate. London Transport tackled this inheritance in the 1950s, with track realignments, resulting in 'empty' platforms appearing at both stations.

That at Gloucester Road is now the Underground's 'Platform for Art' and is used for changing exhibitions (viewed from the present eastbound platform) but South Kensington, which also lost a bay platform in the rebuilding, still has a rather untidy look about it.

WHITE CITY HAMMERSMITH & CITY 1959

Wood Lane Exhibition station, later White City, was opened on 1 May 1908 where the Hammersmith & City Line crosses the A40 Wood Lane. It had a chequered

It is perhaps difficult to reconcile this picture of South Acton station with a separate branch coming from behind the photographer to a terminus on the left of the present tracks, but so it was. The station buildings were adjacent to the existing ticket office building for the North London Line trains of London Overground, with the tracks at a slightly higher level. The London Transport branch saw its last train in 1959. The Richmond to Stratford train was photographed on 4 June 2013. *John Glover*

Acton Town station was reconstructed by Charles Holden into its present form in 1932. That included the provision of a separate and very short branch platform for the South Acton service. On closure of the latter in 1959, the track was removed and an advertisement hoarding was used to screen off the now redundant platform, but little really changed. It is 27 May 2013. *John Glover*

The correction of one of the excesses of competition at South Kensington District Line station, seen here on 27 May 2013, resulted in two platforms now doing the work of the original four. This is the eastbound track, with one of the spare platforms seen to the right. *John Glover*

The sort out of the 1950s at South Kensington also saw the filling in of a surplus east end bay. The resulting gap in the platform awnings can still be seen, while the bay itself is now in part a garden. It is 27 May 2013. *John Glover*

With a similar arrangement to South Kensington, Gloucester Road also had two adjacent stations. Again, the Piccadilly station seen here on 27 May 2013 was later found to be surplus to requirements. *John Glover*

career and tended to be open only when there were exhibitions in progress. It was closed on 24 October 1959 following a fire. Little remains today.

The viaduct location was to the south of the railway bridge over the A40, rather than to the north of it. The latter is where the new Wood Lane station (opened on 17 October 2008) is located. This puts its entrance on the same side of the road as the nearby White City Central Line station.

AMERSHAM TO AYLESBURY

London Underground is not the master of all it surveys; notably there are a number of sections where Underground trains run over Network Rail. Among these are from Queen's Park to Harrow & Wealdstone (Bakerloo) and Gunnersbury to Richmond (District).

The Metropolitan & Great Central Joint Line lost its steam-hauled Underground services north of Amersham on 10 September 1961. Great Missenden is one of those which now rely solely on the offerings of Chiltern Railways and a train for Marylebone is seen here on 11 April 1998. How far is it either reasonable or realistic to project London Underground services outside built up areas, or are these better left to the main line operators? *John Glover*

But there are other places where the Underground has ceased to run. Passenger services are still provided, but by other operators as described in the subsequent sections.

The Metropolitan electrification to Amersham meant that Underground operations further north ceased on 10 September 1961. All services from there to Aylesbury and calling at Wendover, Great Missenden and Stoke Mandeville are now provided by Chiltern Railways. Operation is from London Marylebone, not Baker Street.

EALING BROADWAY

The District Railway reached Ealing Broadway in 1879 and built its own commodious station to the north of the Great Western. By contrast, in 1920 the Central Line was fitted in between with a single island platform.

In a 1966 station building reconstruction, the Underground and main line ticket offices were combined in a new build. The District premises still form an imposing building on the High Street but they are no longer used for railway purposes.

The 1879 District Railway station at Ealing Broadway was a fine affair, and wholly separate from that of the Great Western and the (later) Central Line. A new entrance for all three was opened in 1966 and the District station (at street level) was closed. These are the former railway premises as seen on 27 May 2013. *John Glover*

Above the former Ealing Broadway District Railway station entrance is this pediment still announcing the station name. It was nearly half a century out of date when photographed on 27 May 2013. *John Glover*

A similar rearrangement took place at Highbury & Islington. The construction of the Victoria Line resulted in the Great Northern & City premises dating from 1904 being abandoned.

TOWER HILL

The original Tower of London District Railway station opened in 1882 with the arrival of the line from Aldgate, but it was discarded a couple of years later with the completion of the Circle Line. The new station opened a little further west as Mark Lane on 6 October 1884. It took the more familiar name of Tower Hill on 1 September 1946. The station entrance was located in Byward Street.

It was not however as satisfactory as it might have been, and on 4 February 1967 the Mark Lane site was closed and operations were moved back to the original site on the following day. This too was named Tower Hill.

A major reason for the 1967 change was the ability to build in a terminating platform at the new site. This offered a useful reversing point and avoided overfilling the tracks beyond Aldgate East.

The station bridge within the former Tower Hill (Mark Lane) underground station now forms a pedestrian subway beneath Byward Street. When seen on 24 September 2012 an additional use had been found for it. *John Glover*

45

Unusually, the Mark Lane underground station bridge, which gave access to the two platforms, is still in existence. It is open to the public, forming a subway beneath the road. This might be described as being of a minimal standard. The steps down to the former platforms are closed off, but fitted with shutters for ventilation purposes. No view is possible.

The arrangements on this part of the former station are similar to the entrance to Baker Street on the south side of the Marylebone Road. On the north side the station entrance is still in existence, but hardly recognisable as such.

TRACK SEPARATION

Although the Underground was supposed to be integrated with British Railways, the operational reality was rather different. Separating the two sets of services can be a good reason, as with the Hammersmith & City Line at Paddington.

There are two island platforms, Nos 13/14 and 15/16. The traditional usage was Platform 13 for westbound London Transport trains to Hammersmith and Platform 16 for eastbound services to Whitechapel. British Railways services used Nos 14 and 15 as bays for their terminating local services operated by diesel units.

The disadvantage was that there were a number of conflicting movements for what were both intensive services. The Underground's use of Platform 13 was a particular problem.

The separation of tracks at Paddington main line station obviated a number of conflicting moves, from which everybody gains. This picture of 27 June 1967 shows a Hammersmith bound train of CO/CP stock in Platform 13 and a BR Western Region diesel unit in Platform 15. The platform arrangements are now reversed. *John Glover*

Track rearrangement and resignalling in 1967 separated them completely. London Underground trains henceforth used Platform 15 for their Hammersmith services and Platform 16 for the Whitechapel ones, while British Railways trains had the exclusive use of Nos 13 and 14.

Platform staff now dealt with one operator's services only, while there was no need for signalling equipment to take account of differing systems. The problems of one are now unlikely to affect the other.

The fabric of the station is little changed, but the example shows how modest alterations can make significant changes to station operations.

Hounslow West

Just as Hounslow Town station was found to be in the wrong place, so too was the Hounslow West terminus. Opened for the District Railway in 1884, electric trains reached there on 13 June 1905.

It was reconstructed in Portland stone in a similar style to the Morden extension buildings by Stanley Heaps and Charles Holden, was formally opened on 5 July 1931. This resulted in a station with a ticket hall fronting onto the A3006 Bath Road. Behind there were stairs down to a side platform (right) and an island platform (left). The design allowed for future continuation under the Bath Road.

The polygonal ticket hall of the 1931 reconstruction of Hounslow West by Charles Holden is seen on the left of the picture, with the extended covered walkway thence to the 1975 platforms. It is seen here on 27 May 2013. The former platforms now lie beneath this large car park, but a small part of the canopy for the route down to the most southerly platform can still be discerned. *John Glover*

In the 1970s, an extension to Heathrow Airport was proposed. However, much of the intervening land in the station area had by now been built over, so an underground route which in the first instance kept the railway on the same side of the Bath Road was adopted. This rises to the surface only to cross the River Crane, between Hounslow West and Hatton Cross.

Most unusually, what was built as a completely above ground station now has today's double track formation underground. Construction started east of what was the station throat, taking a more northerly course through a new cutting. At a point equivalent to the eastern end of the platforms on the former line, the new tracks enter a shallow cut-and-cover section, reaching the new station platforms almost immediately. These are of the island type.

This was some distance from the 1931 station building. To enable passengers to cover the intervening distance, which is within the paid area of the station, a totally enclosed covered way was constructed. This leads to steps down to the platform. The somewhat utilitarian structure contrasts with the main building, which still contains the ticket office.

The new platforms were operational from 14 July 1975 and the extension was opened as far as Hatton Cross on 19 July.

The space vacated by the former platforms now forms the station car park.

Harrow & Wealdstone to Watford Junction

There have been no Underground services north of Harrow & Wealdstone to Watford Junction since 24 September 1982 when these stations and the intermediate ones of Headstone Lane, Hatch End, Carpenders Park, Bushey and Watford High Street were last served. Services here are now provided by London Overground from London Euston.

The stations north of Harrow & Wealdstone have not seen a Bakerloo train since 1982. Headstone Lane is one of these and its architecture clearly owes more to the London & North Western Railway than the Underground group. Opened originally on 16 April 1917 as part of the New Line venture, it is seen here on 4 June 2013. *John Glover*

Angel station was reconstructed in 1992. A new northbound platform was built in new tunnelling and the space occupied by the old northbound line (right) was filled in. The result gives the southbound line platform a very spacious appearance. It was photographed on 20 May 2008. *John Glover*

The problem of replacing lifts with escalators Is that either the surface building has to move or the escalators deposit passengers at a different location below ground. In this case, a new surface building was constructed. This is the original, closed in 1992 and now boarded up, seen here on 3 June 2013. *John Glover*

ANGEL

Angel station opened on 17 November 1901 with a narrow island platform, but retained this feature when rebuilt to more generous standards in 1922-24.

Traffic growth made the 12ft wide platform more and more of a liability, especially as all passengers had to make their way to or from its extreme end to reach the stairs which led to the lifts. This could become quite difficult.

The solution was the construction of a new northbound platform in a separate tunnel, with both reached from a new lower concourse at the bottom of a set of escalators. In the old tunnel, the northbound track was removed and the space filled in, with openings in the tunnel wall to allow concourse access. This produced a generous 30ft wide platform tunnel.

At the top of the lower escalators, a passageway leads to the main escalator flight, which with a length of 197ft and a vertical rise of 90ft is the longest on the Underground.

The present station building in Islington High Street was built new in 1992. It is much better situated than the old one in Torrens Street. The latter remains boarded up.

Similar work separating the two tracks each side of an island platform took place at Euston Northern City Line in the 1960s. In 1999 the northbound line at London Bridge was rerouted to create a much larger circulating area, and the same is proposed for Bank.

HILLINGDON

The original Hillingdon opened on 10 December 1923, but in recent times found itself in the path of the A40 Western Avenue rerouting. Consequently, it was rebuilt on a new site a little nearer Uxbridge. The old station closed on 5 December 1992, replaced by the new one on the day after.

Swelling with civic pride, the London Borough of Hillingdon considered the new station to be of architectural importance. It was described as a steel-framed structure with walkways and stairs connecting with a central ticket office. The low-pitched glass roof was stepped down to a lower level on the platforms.

It was awarded Underground Station of the Year, 1992.

This picture of Hillingdon was taken on 8 January 1997; the previous station stood well beyond the end of the present platforms. *John Glover*

BRANCH CLOSURES

Line closures on London Underground are an extremely rare occurrence; that two should happen on the same day was remarkable. It was 30 September 1994.

While a Friday might be considered an unusual choice, neither service by then operated outside the peak hours or at weekends

EPPING-ONGAR

All six ex-Great Eastern Railway stations north of Loughton were transferred from British Railways to London Transport on 25 September 1949. This saw the inauguration of Central Line trains to Epping, but the future of the 6¼-mile section beyond to North Weald, Blake Hall and Ongar remained uncertain. For the time being, British Railways ran a push-pull steam shuttle from Epping on the Underground's behalf.

The Epping-Ongar branch.

Below: The remoteness of Blake Hall station, seen here with a 1962 stock train in March 1977 when it was still open, is all too apparent. Other than the station house, there is little in the way of other sources of rail traffic. Blake Hall was said to have the lowest level of passenger traffic of any metro station in the world, but by any measure this was not an ordinary metro station. *John Glover*

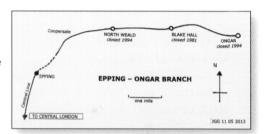

North Weald was a passing place when two-train working was in force, though the loop had been taken out of use by the time of this photograph in March 1977. A train of 1962 stock arrives from Epping heading for Ongar. At least the passengers can console themselves that the branch as a whole lasted until 1994, whereas British Rail services to those rural places such as Buntingford ceased 30 years earlier. *John Glover*

Electrification and operation by the Underground came, eventually, on 18 November 1957. But this was rural territory and traffic levels were always modest. Here, too, the Green Belt legislation made further development unlikely.

The first casualty was the remote Blake Hall station, which closed on 31 October 1981. It was followed by the whole branch, on 30 September 1994.

The railway was sold to the private company Pilot Developments, but little resulted. The line is now owned and operated by Epping Ongar Railway Ltd as a preservation project.

From 2012 the de-electrified railway between Ongar and North Weald stations (only) operates at summer weekends. Services may be projected to Coopersale on a non-alighting basis.

There is no longer any branch access to Epping station, where the two platforms are used by London Underground.

As part of the celebrations for 150 years of London Underground, ex-GWR Prairie 2-6-2T No 5521 was repainted as LT No L150 and used by the Epping Ongar Railway among others. It is seen here at North Weald on 29 June 2013 before departing to Ongar. *John Glover*

Aldwych station was named Strand when it opened on 30 November 1907; its name was changed to Aldwych on 9 May 1915. The station and the branch from Holborn feeding it were closed on 30 September 1994 and since then the station has seen occasional use for filming and similar purposes. The name has also reverted to Strand! It is 25 September 2012. *John Glover*

HOLBORN-ALDWYCH

The Piccadilly was conceived as two separate railways. These were the Great Northern & Strand, from Finsbury Park to Aldwych (formerly Strand) and the Brompton & Piccadilly from the latter to Hammersmith.

In 1901, both came under the control of the American financier Charles Tyson Yerkes. Interests merged and an Act was obtained to link the two, from Holborn via Leicester Square to Piccadilly Circus

That would leave what became the 573yd Aldwych branch from Holborn as a more or less free-standing entity. It was opened on 13 November 1907. The line was closed completely during World War 2 from 1940 to 1946, with the station areas used for various wartime purposes.

A post-war feature was the installation of a bell push on the Holborn platform, which rang a bell in the lift at Aldwych. The guard pressed this as the train was about to leave Holborn and the lift at Aldwych was then started. Passengers arrived on the platform at the same time as the train.

The branch led a precarious existence as a self-contained single track line, with modest passenger numbers. Latterly operating peak hours only, by the early 1990s the expense of lift renewal could be avoided no longer. It closed for good on 30 September 1994.

The Aldwych branch is no longer part of the operational railway, but it is retained for non-passenger use. Track, signals and infrastructure are kept in running order and a train of 1972 Mk1 stock is kept on the branch for use in commercial filming.

CHARING CROSS

The Jubilee Line was conceived as a separation of the two branches of what was the Bakerloo Line. The Jubilee would become a self-contained operation from Stanmore over new construction from Baker Street to Charing Cross with intermediate stations at Bond Street and Green Park. This formed Stage 1 of a grander project, which could have seen what was originally termed the Fleet Line extended to the City and then Lewisham. Later this was replaced by the River Line to Thamesmead and Beckton.

The line from Baker Street to Charing Cross and its platforms opened on 1 May 1989 and all was well for a time. The tracks continued beyond the station as an over-run as far as the north end of Waterloo Bridge.

Then came the revival of Docklands, which suggested a demand and hence an alignment further south. After intense debate, not least on its funding, the Jubilee Line Extension to Stratford via Westminster, Waterloo, London Bridge and Canary Wharf was completed in late 1999.

If Westminster and Waterloo were to be included, routeing via Charing Cross was impractical. With a new junction south of Green Park, the original Charing Cross terminal became redundant and closed on 19 November 1999. The former line from Green Park remains available for operational use, but there is no public access.

That Charing Cross Jubilee Line station could be built on a new line from Green Park and opened in 1979, and then closed completely in 1999, shows just how fast the rebirth of London Docklands took place. This view of 1972 MkII stock, now operating on the Bakerloo only, was taken at the Charing Cross terminus. The line remains in situ, but there is no public access. *John Glover*

The 21st Century

The present century has seen a huge increase in Underground and indeed National Rail patronage, and there have been many schemes designed to cope with additional passenger volumes.

FULHAM BROADWAY

The District Railway station at Fulham Broadway opened on 1 March 1880 as Walham Green. It was rebuilt by the railway's Harry W Ford in 1905 to cater for increasing business, especially crowds attending the nearby Stamford Bridge football ground.

The tracks are below road level and the southern approach is tunnelled. The entrance led to a wide corridor and footbridge access to the two side platforms. These have a fine overall roof.

The station was given its present name on 2 March 1952,

In 2003 that entrance was closed, replaced by one some way east along the same Fulham Road. Intending passengers have to run the gauntlet of a shopping centre to access the station, but once inside much is as before. At platform level the roof survives, but the open section beyond (to the north) is now overlaid by part of the shopping centre. There is a new side exit to the Fulham ground, a considerable improvement.

The original entrance is Grade 1 listed and is now in commercial non-railway premises.

CITY WIDENED LINES: KING'S CROSS TO MOORGATE

The Widened Lines were a creation of the Metropolitan Railway, and introduced what amounted to a four-track section from King's Cross to Farringdon, Barbican and Moorgate. They offered running connections to the Great Northern and the Midland railways at King's Cross and St Pancras, and the opportunity to cross the river via Farringdon to Blackfriars and the Chatham company's lines. Paddington was already connected to the Metropolitan.

This was primarily for goods traffic and there were four such terminals en route. It also gave useful City access for passenger trains, latterly those of the Great Northern and Midland.

Later, the physical connections between the Widened Lines and the main Underground network were severed, as was the link south of the river. Great Northern services by this route ceased with their 1976 electrification, though those to the Midland continued with the electrification in 1983.

Above: This is the District Railway's entrance to Fulham Broadway station, which is situated on Fulham Road. This is a Grade II listed building, closed in 2003 and turned over to commercial uses. A new station entrance was created further east. This photograph was taken on 1 June 2009. *John Glover*

Right: The disused Widened Lines terminal platforms at Moorgate were spruced up for the London Underground 150 celebrations, albeit not used for such. They are seen here on 3 June 2013. The shaft through which daylight reaches the now almost totally enclosed station was provided to disperse the exhaust from the diesel traction at one time used on these services. *John Glover*

Right: National Rail services on the Widened Lines ceased on 20 March 2009, in order to allow platform lengthening at Farringdon to take place. At Barbican on 3 June 2013, all traces of the overhead electrification have been removed, the grass is growing and stop blocks are in place. The depredations of World War 2 saw the overall roof dismantled, though the supports are still visible. Underground services call at the other two platforms. *John Glover*

The new S stock of London Underground will operate all sub-surface Underground services in due course, but the first line to be fully equipped was the Metropolitan. However, since the S stock trains operate as single units, there is no opportunity for splitting them, with the result that Chesham, where a four-car train of A stock was perfectly adequate to run the shuttle service to Chalfont & Latimer, is now served by eight-car trains of S stock. But the bay at Chalfont, seen here on 14 September 2008, was not long enough. This results in all Chesham trains running to and from Baker Street or Aldgate, with the Chalfont bay now disused. *John Glover*

The Midland's became part of the Thameslink operation with the restoration of the link to Blackfriars from 16 May 1988. Moorgate was still served, but only at peak.

The King's Cross Thameslink station was closed on 8 December 2007, services being transferred to the low level platforms at St Pancras. What remained of the Underground platforms here had been disused since 1941 when the Metropolitan station was rebuilt on a new site.

Thameslink operation to Moorgate ended on 20 March 2009 to enable platforms at Farringdon to be lengthened to take 12 cars. The Widened Lines platforms at Barbican and Moorgate thus became physically isolated. They are likely to stay that way, unless London Underground can find a constructive use for them.

EAST LONDON LINE

From the earliest days of operation on the East London Line, some were provided by constituent companies of what became London Transport. On nationalisation in 1948, the line was vested in that organisation. It then offered a through route from Liverpool Street to what was then the Southern Region of British Railways. Latterly, it became a stub end Underground operation only, from Shoreditch to Whitechapel and New Cross or New Cross Gate (often abbreviated to NX/NXG).

With some interruptions, this continued until 22 December 2007 when the line was closed completely. Large-scale investment allowed the new services of London

Shoreditch station was most awkwardly placed in railway network terms, and it was of no surprise that the proposed development and conversion of the East London Line to London Overground operation saw its closure. The station building was at ground level, with what was latterly a single platform in a cutting deep below. It was closed permanently on 9 June 2006. This photograph was taken when it had a year or two left, on 16 June 2003. *John Glover*

London Underground kept Shoreditch station in good condition, but what happens following closure is the concern of others. This was the scene on 23 March 2012. *John Glover*

Overground to be extended north of Whitechapel on new construction to a Shoreditch High Street station and on to Highbury & Islington using initially the old Broad Street railway viaduct.

To the south, services are continued from New Cross Gate to West Croydon, Crystal Palace and Clapham Junction. Most of the extensions are over Network Rail owned track and operation is now by London Overground using third-rail dc traction.

The construction of the road bridge at an oblique angle over the East London Line at Surrey Quays makes an unusual platform level feature. It is seen here on 4 June 2013. Services to two destinations in the north and four in the south are now provided exclusively by London Overground. London Underground operations ceased on 22 December 2007. *John Glover*

This is a platform level view of Rotherhithe, the East London line station, on 26 April 2006. This was before London Underground gave up operation; it is now part of London Overground. This view looks south towards Surrey Quays, away from the original Brunel tunnel under the Thames. *John Glover*

As a consequence, the old Shoreditch station, which latterly consisted of a single low-level platform between retaining walls, was closed permanently on 9 June 2006. The station opened originally on 10 April 1876, but it had become a dead end in railway terms. The replacement Shoreditch High Street station opened on 27 April 2010 as did the core of the new Overground operation.

WATFORD (METROPOLITAN)

The branch from Moor Park to Watford, commonly known as Watford (Met), was opened on 2 November 1925. This was a joint Metropolitan/LNER venture and there was one intermediate station at Croxley.

The aim was Watford itself and the railway was built with the station buildings on a bridge over the tracks, but extension never came. The company was thwarted by the environmentalists of the day, who didn't want the tracks crossing Cassiobury

Park. The result was that the Metropolitan terminus is surrounded by a modest number of houses in a location a good half-mile short of the town centre.

For the last two decades there have been proposals to divert this line to link it with what remains of the Croxley Green LNWR branch. This would give the Metropolitan direct access to Watford High Street and Watford Junction stations, sharing the tracks presently used by London Overground. Additional stations are to be Cassio Bridge on the entirely new section and Watford Vicarage Road on the former Croxley Green branch. The present Watford (Met) terminus would be closed.

With funding already agreed, on 24 July 2013 the works received Ministerial consent and the Mayor of London indicated his agreement to the consequential closure of Watford (Met) station.

Completion by 2016 is anticipated.

The Metropolitan's Watford terminus of 1925 was built with the intention of the line continuing to Watford Town Centre, but this was not to be. It is seen here on 14 September 2008. The architect of this spacious station constructed in a domestic style was the Metropolitan's Charles Walter Clark. *John Glover*

Conclusions

As demonstrated, Underground stations can be 'lost' for many reasons. These range from outright closure to extensive rebuilding on a new site or transfer to another operator. Many such changes are beneficial to passengers.

These processes will continue as the system is further updated and expanded. There will also be a greater integration with the National Rail network. Crossrail 1, Thameslink and (perhaps) Crossrail 2 are examples.

More Lost Stations

There are two more 'stations' which deserve mention. The 'Chelsea Monster' was a name bequeathed to the Lots Road Power Station when it was built in 1905 for the Metropolitan District Electric Traction Co (MDET). It is on the north bank of the Thames, adjacent to the bridge carrying the West London line of National Railways. When built, it was said to be the largest power station in the world, supplying electric traction to the Underground companies and tramways. It consumed 700 tons of coal a day and was later converted to fuel oil, then gas. The four chimneys were reduced to two.

Despite updating from time to time, Lots Road was closed on 21 October 2002 and sold to a developer. The Underground now takes its power from the National Grid.

The other form of 'station' is that used when the ordinary station is closed during engineering works. Bus replacement services are usual, but where should an intending passenger stand to wait for them? Recent times have seen ordinary bus stops suitably adorned, or temporary stops put in place. Do these also count as 'stations', and if so is the one they replace 'lost' for the time being?

The author hopes that this book will have been of interest to the reader. It does not and cannot cover all possible examples; the emphasis has been on those where there is something for the casual observer to see or an interesting story to be told. The photographs are scenes of places to which the public has access.

The stopping places for rail replacement bus services were never identified other than by the presence of an official, but bus stops, temporary or permanent, have appropriate markings. This one was at Leytonstone, Central Line, on 19 June 2003. *John Glover*

Below: The Chelsea Monster was the local name for Lots Road Power Station, which in its time generated electricity for most of the London Transport undertaking's operations. It is situated on the north bank of the Thames just below Chelsea (railway) bridge and was photographed on 22 April 2009. *John Glover*

Index